B.A.D.D HABITS

Brittany Parker

ISBN: 978-1-09837-340-5

BUILDING AND DELIVERING DREAMS

The woman I am today I didn't become overnight. In all honesty, it was the need to overcome my own insecurities and failures that ultimately motivated me and gave me strength. This book has been in the making now for about five years. I'd start, stop, become sidetracked, and before I knew it, it was just another clever idea I once had but let fade away. The second-guessing and the not believing in myself started to get the best of me. *Who am I? Who cares to hear my story? You're wasting your time, Britt.* These were the thoughts that ran through my head, but I realized it was just the devil trying to prevent me from sharing my story and my many testimonies.

However, just as with everything else in life, the devil had control only temporarily. God is the author of my life, and it wasn't long before I realized the delay was simply because my story had just begun. My platform wasn't big enough; I was minimizing the big screen. God's plans for my life were bigger and came with a twist that I still sometimes can't believe. I was standing in the way and blocking my blessings. Once I understood I was planting my seeds in dirt, but it was the fertilizer that I needed to get those nutrients, life began to look up for me. It's not forgetting our past but recognizing our mistakes that makes us better human beings. To say that I would not have done things differently isn't completely true, yet I don't regret my journey. Understanding my path was necessary to get to this space of growth in my life. I'm thankful for patience, peace, and clarity to finally birth these dreams.

Beginning to an End

Proverbs 3:5–7: Trust in the LORD with all thine heart; and lean not unto thine own understanding. In all thy ways acknowledge him, and he shall direct thy paths. Be not wise in thine own eyes: fear the LORD, and depart from evil.

This was the first scripture I memorized as a child. Who knew how important this scripture would be to me and how much I'd rely on it throughout life? Success doesn't have a time frame. It takes some of us longer, yet there is no expiration date. Early I knew I wanted to get married, have kids, and live the perfect life like the one the Cosby family displayed on television. I had everything planned out and no one could tell me anything. I was popular and a social butterfly in high school who was involved in many activities. Life was already paved for me—there was no way I wouldn't succeed. I remember my parents and other adults telling my friends and me not to rush our teenage years, to enjoy them while we could. I was such a know-it-all I couldn't wait to graduate and be free because I was positive I'd blend right in once I entered the real world.

In the fall of 2003, I moved to Tallahassee to start the next phase of my life, college. I was now a student at Florida Agricultural and

Mechanical University, better known as FAMU, and I'd waited for this moment for what seemed like an eternity. Going to college was always the plan for me. I'd been a part of college-based programs since I was in the sixth grade. The first program I joined was College Reach Out and I remained in this program until high school. During my eleventh grade year, I moved up to Upward Bound, which was more in depth yet a great experience. One would think as long as I'd been a part of these college preparation programs I would have hit the ground running once I stepped foot on campus. However, attending college was a shock for me.

Being on my own and away from my parents, having a room-mate, and being around thousands of strangers brought new experiences I wasn't keen on. Someone who was in such a rush to be a young adult was now like a frightened child. Yes, I had friends who attended FAMU with me; I even had friends over at Florida State. However, this wasn't enough, and I didn't feel confident. The FAMU gospel choir, church, Bethel's restaurant, and in my friend's dorm room were where you could find me. The harsh reality was that I couldn't wait to be a college student, but now that I was there I couldn't wait to leave. I went home every weekend and ultimately that was my downfall. I didn't give myself a chance to adjust to the university or to Tallahassee. Tallahassee was too country and I compared it to Tampa repeatedly. Once I'd created those negative thoughts in my head, I was convinced and there was no turning back. I knew when I went home for Christmas break I wouldn't return.

B.A.D.D HABITS 101: Once you graduate high school and turn eighteen, real life begins. Whether you get a job, go to college, join the army, or even take the first year off to figure out what you really want to do with your life, you eventually have to make a decision. The misconception that young students have when they graduate high school is that things are easy. They are not. Having to spread your wings before knowing you can fly sometimes is a harsh reality. Regardless of your upbringing or how well you may have been raised, nothing prepares you for life like experience. Many young people adjust well, but many struggle. Coming from a big city like Tampa to a country town like Tallahassee, I felt sheltered. It's like my light was being dimmed and Tallahassee just didn't give me the limelight I'd envisioned. Yet when I'd go home on the weekends to hang out with friends and party, I'd have the time of my life. When I'd go back to Tallahassee, I felt as if I was depriving myself and that I was missing out on "the life." With my mindset back then, I just wasn't ready for college even with the years spent preparing. I wanted to be an adult, but I really just wanted to do whatever I wanted. College is great if you are ready, but you have to be ready. Neither your parents nor your friends can want it for you. College offers different environments, good experiences, and opportunities, but it is up to you to create them. For some students, the college years are the best years of their lives—I wanted to end college before it began. Parents should talk with their kids who are going off to college to find out if they're ready. You can tell a lot about a child's personality and maturity by the grades he or she makes in high school. As an older nontraditional student who has classes with many younger students, I see myself in so many of them. They have no drive, they don't want to put in the work, they're simply just there. While I can only provide encouragement, it's evident college is not meant for everyone. Knowing your place in the world is a necessity.

Accountability

It wasn't long before I realized being an adult suck. I was not home a year and I was already pregnant with my first child. Young, foolish, and carefree, I was now a mother but had no sense of responsibility. I knew my family had my back and always having a way out was my downfall. Three years later, I was pregnant with my second child. Work was inconsistent. This was the life I'd created for myself, and while it was not the life I'd planned, things were what they were. How could this be? I knew the answer to this question, but I wasn't ready to face it.

I can be real with myself now and admit I was lost and just moving through life with no real direction. The immature mindset I had at the time was that I was okay, and I made myself believe I was doing enough when I knew I wasn't. Life doesn't come with instructions; when you make your bed, you must lie in it. I was the mother of two kids, yet I lived my life like it was Jumanji. I was having fun and carefree. Life had its ups and downs, good and bad, and everything in between. In the middle of so much inconsistency I convinced myself I was on still on my A game, that this was the way life should be and no one can judge me.

I was grown and didn't care how others perceived me. In my twenties, my thought process was if I were going to make mistakes, this was the time. Everything was trial and error. I hadn't experienced life enough to solidify who I was. No one was perfect and perfect wasn't going to start with me. However, as time progressed, I began facing reality. Seeing the life that was versus what life could be provided the light I needed. I wasn't doing enough and there was no other way around it. It was time to take action—no one else was going to do it for me. Change was key.

B.A.D.D HABITS 101: We can all look at life and blame others for things that happened or didn't happen, what a person did to us, the predicament they placed us in, and the list goes on. However, taking accountability for your part in the situation is all that matters. You can change no one but yourself. Finding faults in others does nothing to cure you. When you are placed in situations that are not suitable for you, figure out your part as it relates to making things better and move forward. Playing the blame game and holding grudges only leaves you frustrated. I realized that I play a part in anything that transpires in my life. I recognized that I always have a choice. I can't change things that have been done, but I can change how I proceed, and that's the shift I made. I did, I allowed, I can, and I will move forward. I've had accountability partners and I've been one. Get people in your life who can be honest enough with you to tell you where you are lacking, where you aren't doing right or enough. You are responsible for yourself and the things that happen in your life, period.

Done Doubting

Now thirty-one and going through a divorce, I no longer allowed any further downfalls I had to define me. My thought process was to get back to the old me, but I before I could get back to me, I had to find who I was. I was just a child playing grown-up games. I hadn't established an identity. The time was now to use my shortcomings and build a better future. I realized the real world wasn't set to baby me and that if I wanted success it was my own responsibility. It wasn't until I reached my early thirties that I was able to grasp the concept of life. "I used to be this" and "I did that" were irrelevant and it was time to tap into the real Brittany. My parents gave me all the love they should, yet no one else owed me anything. I had to take the lemons I'd thrown myself and mix them with a little tea. I refused to make any more excuses—this was all about learning and restoring myself. My family would always ask me when I was going to go back to school, but I'd quickly switch the subject because that was a conversation I just wasn't ready to visit. Unbeknownst to me, things were about to take a turn that even I didn't foresee.

In October 2016, my kids and I went on a trip with my parents to FAMU's homecoming. I hadn't been back to Tallahassee since I'd left FAMU in 2003. It felt so good to be away and show my kids my life before they were conceived. I felt refreshed and free. I remember asking my kids if they would want to move up to Tallahassee, and they quickly answered yes. After we'd come home from an amazing weekend, I didn't waste time calling the admissions office to see what the deadline was to apply for the spring 2017 semester. Unfortunately, I'd just missed the deadline by two weeks. A glimpse of hope I had quickly faded away, or at least that's the way it seemed. I spoke and God heard me; it was time to let him lead.

Not letting this stop me, I enrolled at Hillsborough Community College (HCC) in January 2017. I knew it wouldn't be easy, but this was a fresh start for me and I was ready. Giving 100 percent and nothing less was all that it could be from that point on. The excitement of starting back to school took over the fears I had of being out so long and not succeeding.

My family and friends were a huge support for me in being the stage and the audience I needed. As far as my job went, I was now looking to have life accommodate me while I provided for myself and my children. I remember leaving corporate America in March 2016. I left a job where I was making almost $17.00 an hour for a job with the school district making $10.50. People told me I was crazy and wondered why I would make such a decision. The answer for me was simple. I needed to be available for my kids. I would not have to pay for health insurance because the school district covered employees, and I would work five minutes away from home rather than thirty (which saved me gas). I no longer had to pay for after school care because I got off at 3:30 p.m., and if I needed to pick my kids up and bring them to my job, it was never an issue. When you have kids, there are certain things that money can't buy or replace. The school district provided security for me in ways that corporate America could not. Making more money didn't help me. It hurt me as the more money I made, the more I spent. As crazy as it sounds, I was actually able to save more money when I made less. I was no longer chasing money so much that I hated getting up to go make it every morning. Balance was the new play for my game and money wasn't going to define me.

B.A.D.D HABITS 101: We are our own worst critics at times. I can't speak for anyone else, but the fear of failure has prevented me from doing many things. The what ifs, the who doesn't, and the whys and why nots have always gotten the best of me. You will never know if you will succeed if you never try. At times my dilemma was worrying about what others had to say or how they perceived me. I had to get to the point of just doing me. People will talk regardless, whether you're doing good or bad. The capabilities God gave me are just for me. Before anyone can believe in you, you have to believe in yourself. Move without doubt. Know that you can do all things through Christ or whomever your higher power may be who strengthens you. No need to fret. You've got this.

Dominate

Things were going great, and life was looking up for myself and my kids. I was now creating a life of substance, and while those stepping-stones may have seemed small to some, they were wins for me. I was with the school board for a year, and then I transitioned to a new position with better pay. Months later, that same position opened up at an elementary school, which now gave me the summers off. This experience was life changing for me. God's timing is never wrong, and when he placed me at this school, he blessed me both mentally and physically. I was able to form a bond and gain an extended family with some of the staff and faculty members I worked with. You never know what you need until you have things at your fingertips, and at this time in my life, they were all necessary. I felt overwhelmed at times, like it was me against the world, so it was nice to be around those who cared, made me laugh, and encouraged me. While I liked my job, it didn't take me long to realize the lack of support from the higher-ups. I was working for a school district where education is key, yet the district didn't offer tuition assistance or reimbursement programs for the staff. Feeling unappreciated as an employee, I let my frustrations begin to get the best of me, and I even tested those I had close bonds with.

Things were going so right; I didn't need anything to go wrong. The reality was that I was getting anxious knowing I should be doing so much more, and I felt complacent. I remember sitting at my desk one day just completely over it. I sat quietly that day because I knew my time was winding down and I could no longer fake being happy in my position. My work sisters advised me to go home early that day because they could sense something was off with me. I cried all the way home. *Lord, I just need a breakthrough.* Having the same breaks and time off as my kids was no longer good enough, and while my job was easy, it was all it was ever going to be. I was now stuck with the tough decision of accepting things as they were or leaving.

I found myself going back to the question of who I am, and what I came up with I didn't like. Critique from within is harder than criticism from without: b-bold, r-rude, i-ignorant at times, t-temperamental, t-tolerance zero, a-anxious, n-not so nice, and y-yearning for more. Desperate and on edge, I started applying for jobs I knew I'd hate but that offered great money. For the moment, that was enough for me, or was it? I now found myself backtracking to what I'd originally said I wasn't going to do, taking better pay knowing it would only satisfy me temporarily. I was headed toward making the wrong decisions; it was definitely time to pray.

B.A.D.D HABITS 101: Being controlling can be a negative attribute, but taking control of your life is a positive one. When life comes at you hard, your response has to be aggressive. No matter how hard your situation seems, never show weakness. There were plenty of days I wanted to give up, and some days it took everything in me to smile. Yet I refused defeat. I had to dominate my situation, to grip life with all I had. I didn't have any more years to sit back and wait. The race had begun and I was ready to win. If you want to succeed, you have to know that your competition is you. A million people can sell the same product or be in the same line of business, but they will never be you. You control your circumstances.

Higher

God finally spoke to me. Two years after I originally talked about going back to FAMU to finish what I had started, I looked to apply for the fall 2018 semester. This time around I hadn't missed the deadline and had about three weeks. Still at HCC, I'd already slowed down my class intake and had planned to transfer. While everything else seemed closed, this path had a green light. From the time I decided I was going back to FAMU, everything fell into place. My prayers hadn't fallen on deaf ears after all. God was just shaking me and testing my faith. Because the transition wasn't just me and I was now bringing two kids along, a lot had to go into this move with no time to waste. Because I knew I couldn't have any delays and one wrong move could throw me off, I made a few trips so that I could find answers and get things done face-to-face. Everything paid off, and I was admitted as a returning student.

Within a month and a half, I packed up our belongings and moved to Tallahassee. Things happened so quickly I didn't have time to rest. The adrenaline rush I had from these new beginnings was all the energy I needed. I had so much business to handle and so little time. Though I'd been accepted back into FAMU and my transfer GPA from HCC was over a 2.0, I still had to file a financial aid appeal because when I had left FAMU, my GPA was a 1.3. I turned in all of the required documentation over the summer and was ready to start. In August, my appeal was denied. *Lord, if it's not one thing it's another.* I wasn't planning to pay for school out of pocket, so I began panicking. I kept reminding myself I had uprooted my kids—this couldn't be the final decision. I called the financial aid office, and immediately the person I spoke with said the committee only meets once and they don't usually do appeals. I would have to wait until spring 2019.

Not taking no for an answer, I asked for the names of managers and vice-president and began to send emails. After finally getting in contact with the right person, I was told my appeal wasn't specific and to resubmit the application with more information. I sent in the documentation that same day, and this time it was approved. This was such a tedious and aggravating process I told myself to make sure I would never have to do it again.

I'd already planned to not work the first semester and just be a full-time student. I wanted to make sure the kids were settled and acclimated in the new environment and that everything went smoothly. This time around things were going to be different. I was going in prepared and open to all opportunities. I ended up getting a job in the bookstore, which was very different for me. I needed to get acquainted not only with the school but with new people. Life had humbled me, and I was not going to take anything for granted. Although I only worked there for a short time, I accomplished my mission. I met some great people and grew familiar with the school. I was now in my comfort zone, something I had never felt the first time.

B.A.D.D HABITS 101: The good thing about life is that no matter how many times you fall, you can get back up and try again. We are all students of life. What we desire and the paths we want determine the lengths to which we're willing to go. I'd learned how to accept and be accountable for my life. I did not need anyone to tell me I wasn't doing enough—at this point the feeling was second nature. All of my hopes and dreams were attainable. I just had to go get them. I was looking to be higher in every aspect of my life. You can reach your destiny; don't be afraid of heights.

Attainable

I remember calling my dad on the first day of class so that he could talk to me while I was on my way to class. I was like a little kid on the first day of school, extremely nervous. It was hot and I was tired. Having to walk up all those hills was something I definitely had to get used to again. Being surrounded by other students just like me trying to get to class felt like I was in a twilight zone. As I was walking, I observed the scenery and it was so different. Certainly it was not the FAMU I attended back in 2003, where it was a daily fashion show. These students dressed so freely and comfortably, which wasn't a bad thing. I got through my first class and I could breathe. The second class started and I had anxiety all over again. The professor began by having us write down our name, where we're from, and something interesting about ourselves. I contemplated what to write. I didn't really want to talk, and I didn't want to be the old student in the class, but I had promised myself to be open this time and not an introvert. When my turn came to introduce myself to the class, I was a nervous wreck.

"Hello. My name is Brittany Randall and I'm from Tampa. Something interesting about me is that this is my second time around at FAMU. I first attended when I graduated high school in 2003. I have two kids and this is my second chance." I quickly sat down and the class applauded me. I was not looking for applause, but that moment alone was a breakthrough for me. After class, the professor said, "I knew you were older than the other students, but I didn't think you were that much older. You'll be fine; this time will go by quickly."

I took four classes my first semester back and I finally got into the swing of things. I communicated with my classmates and some of my professors leaned on me when it came to bigger responsibilities. I felt confident and at peace. The Tallahassee that was too country for me fourteen years' prior had become my sanity. Tallahassee was a great place to raise a family. It didn't take my kids long at all to make friends and get involved with activities, and that made me happy. Their success was just as important as mine because we were a team. Making the sacrifice of moving one hundred miles per hour at times was one I was willing to make to ensure they weren't deprived as I chased my dreams at age thirty-three.

The semester was over and I ended with A's, B's, and one C. Shocked and disappointed in the C as I think I was only two points away from a B, I quickly got over it as I was just glad that I'd passed the semester and pleased to see my GPA rise to over a 2.0. Now it was time to get down to business and start applying for jobs. All I can say is "whew, what a time!" I'd started in December in what felt like a never-ending situation. I applied to more than fifty jobs and it took a month and a half before I started getting calls back.

The process was very slow and had me questioning myself and my skills. I'd started getting interviews and invitations to take assessments, but the ratio of available positions to applicants was insane and overwhelming, to say the least.

B.A.D.D HABITS 101: Your dreams are attainable. Set up a plan. Success doesn't happen overnight; while it sometimes comes faster for others, it doesn't happen in a day. Whatever you set out to achieve can be done. Be realistic with yourself. Set goals that can be accomplished within reason and with time. Remember things that come easy don't last long, and slow and steady always wins the race. When others say you can't, show them why you can.

Building

Spring classes began and I was still looking for employment. Here it was March and I wasn't working. I was starting to get depressed. My savings were running low, and I asked God to come through. Panicked but still praying, I didn't quit. In April, I finally started getting second interviews and things began to look up. I was so excited to be getting closer to working, yet the downside was that the hiring process took so long that it would still be another month before I could start. Finally, I received my first job offer. After the first one, the offers began to pour in. At my fourth job offer, I'd made my decision. I signed the paperwork so the background check could begin.

A few days later, I received a phone call about that position, and the secretary stated the head manager wanted me to come back in for a follow-up interview. I was confused because I'd already been offered the position, but I'd never worked in Tallahassee, so I thought maybe this was protocol. When I arrived, I was seated in a room with two managers. The head director began to explain why they'd called me back in. She stated that when they conducted my reference checks with my previous employer, they spoke with one of my old bosses who told them that they wouldn't rehire me. The energy that went through my body was indescribable.

The head director asked me to listen to her before I spoke. She explained that normally after a reference check like that, they pulled the job offer and moved to the next candidate. They had called me in to get my side because none of them had received that energy from me.

This was nobody but God. These people didn't know me from a can of paint, but they were open to hearing me out before going with a "credible source." I first explained how shocked I was and then responded to the foolish claims. After I had finished speaking, she told me that we could move forward if I could get another reference. Getting a reference wasn't a problem as I knew the principal I had worked for had marked me as someone who could be rehired. However, the embarrassment I felt got the best of me. Imagine new coworkers whom you've not yet started working with getting a tarnished perception of you based off of someone else.

I didn't make it out of the building before tears started rolling down my face. I felt so sabotaged. I remember having a conference call with my friends and family members and telling them, and they were in disbelief. The old Brittany wanted to call the person who had given that negative reference, but I already had what I needed and there was no reason to worry. At that point, my reputation was on the line, and to me that was the bigger issue. I went over and beyond what they asked of me. I even called some of my old coworkers and friends from the high school. Everyone I called vouched for me without hesitation. I was also able to get a copy of the letter about rehiring me and all was well. This situation was just a reminder that people are envious. People see a promising future in us that sometimes we ourselves don't see. I was made to succeed and not fail. This was just an added reason to go hard and excel.

B.A.D.D HABITS 101: Before you can build, there must be a solid foundation. Order your steps and know that every step taken prepares you for the next. When you're the builder, you can create things exactly how you want them because you are the architect of your life. Attention to detail, rapport, and creating healthy relationships along the way are great tools when building for success. If you aren't strong enough, you can be torn down. Be Ford tough: love and create in ways that can't be broken.

Initiative

The spring semester ended and I made the honor roll. My kids were doing well and I was waiting to start my new job. After receiving the rehire letter and speaking with my other references, the manager called me back and told me they were proceeding with the hiring process. Now I could breathe and relax until my start date.

One day, I was sitting at home and my phone rang. The call was coming from the 850 area code, and though I'd been in Tallahassee almost a year, when someone with that area code called, it was still strange to see. I knew it wasn't the kids' school, so I was unsure of who it could be. I answered with hesitation only to find myself speaking with a human resources representative from FAMU about a job I'd applied for. I heard the lady talking, but I was honestly thrown off. I was so focused on trying to remember which job I had applied for and when that I didn't catch her name. She asked me to come in for an interview. I said I was done with interviews and that I was sticking with a job offer I'd already accepted, especially since they'd gone to bat for me. But jobs are businesses, and at the end of the day I always have to do what's best for me. I was a little reluctant, but I figured it couldn't hurt anything to go on the interview.

I thought about how this opportunity could work for me. The kids were attending FAMU DRS, and I was a student at FAMU. To work on campus would be perfect. I didn't think things could get more solid than this. When I went in for the interview, three interviewers were sitting inside the room. Still to this day I don't know why, but to say I was nervous is an understatement. I couldn't speak. I was fumbling over my words, and I just knew I'd blown it. After the interview, I took an assessment, and at that point I figured it didn't matter how I did. These people weren't going to hire me. When I finished the assessment and walked out, all I could say was, "Thank you, Lord, for the other position."

Later that week, I checked my email and I saw that the supervisor who had interviewed me from FAMU had emailed me about a second interview. Completely shocked, I quickly called to confirm my availability for that interview. I already had a job, but this position paid more and it just wouldn't get more convenient than to work on campus. That next Tuesday I had my second interview, and I was actually supposed to start my job with the state in three days. I let the supervisor know up front that I had accepted another job offer, but if she could let me know their decision as soon as possible, I'd accept the position if it were offered. The following morning, FAMU called and offered me the job. I was so excited; I couldn't believe it. I'd gone all around Tallahassee interviewing for jobs, going to places and areas I never knew existed. This job with FAMU was one of the first jobs I had applied to yet I'd heard nothing. God really brought me full circle just to show me that things are done in his perfect timing.

While I hated to call the other job and decline the position, again it was just business and I had to do what was best for me. I started my new job and I loved the environment. It was laid back, the people were friendly, and I discovered some perks I didn't know about when I accepted the position. The university closes for a week at Christmas, which gives employees basically two weeks off with the weekends. Again, God saw my need and wrote his plan perfectly. In Tallahassee, with some friends but no family, I needed to be as flexible as possible. Most holidays I had off with the kids, and the school paid for six credit hours a semester. The job also provided good pay—all I had searched for back home was laid out for me in little Tallahassee.

B.A.D.D HABITS 101: You can't always depend on others. There are times when you need to take the initiative. I've learned that waiting on others to do things puts you on their time, which may not be a rush. Whatever you want you can have, but you must go get it. Taking the initiative is a great quality. It shows you're a leader, a go-getter who get can get the job done.

The Time Is Now

Life is good today. I have married an awesome guy who like me isn't from Tallahassee, but different reasons led us to the city. He also works for FAMU and we share so many similarities. Such a breath of fresh air, this man has swept me off my feet. He is a true go-getter and shares my attitude of living life to the fullest. Harold met my parents, my kids, and my other family members, and they approved. With family being so important and us being so close-knit, it was important that he fit in. My kids like him, and I can honestly say I've met the man of my dreams.

God has given me another chance. I'm taking summer classes and now I feel like a professional student. Unlike the first time around, I'm now into my third semester and I finally feel like I belong. I'm interacting in every class and even talking and answering more than my classmates. A few of them ask me for assistance and I feel honored. I am no smarter than the next person, yet the leader in me still shines where others can see and that's a compliment for me. I'm in a good place with myself, my kids are good, I'm in a great relationship, and there is no other place I'd rather be.

When I first started back at FAMU in the fall of 2018, I gave myself two years. I was set on graduating in the fall of 2020. I didn't take any semesters off, I stayed enrolled full time, and I even took classes each summer. However, I realized it would be too much pressure on me to fulfill that demand, and so spring 2021 was the reality. I was a little disappointed, yet I had to see all I had on my plate and understand that it was okay. It was just one semester longer, and it would be here before I knew it. Delayed never meant denied, and I needed to give myself a break. I'd come so far and small victories should be basked in and celebrated.

In December 2019, life took another great turn. Harold proposed to me. I was so excited as I have had no doubt in my mind that he is the right man for me from the first day we met. At this point in my life things were clear and nothing that had transpired in my life was by accident. It wasn't about how I started but how I finished. I'd only come to Tallahassee to obtain my bachelor's degree, but I was reaping so much more. In this season, I wasn't questioning or overthinking. I was deserving of everything that was taking place in my life and it felt great.

Now that Harold and I were engaged, it was time to plan a fabulous wedding. We hired coordinators, booked our venue, and contacted food and cake vendors, and then we were brought to a halt. COVID-19 was here and it wasn't disappearing. Although we were hopeful it would pass, we quickly began to realize that, like many other engaged couples, we were at risk of not being able to have a wedding. Not wanting to waste any more money or time, we decided to have a small ceremony and married seven months early. This was not the plan, but the ceremony turned out beautifully. It was small, intimate, and cost-efficient. Other than the fact that some important people were not able to make it, it was perfect. Since my husband and I started dating, we have done everything on our own time and in our own way. While some of our qualities are traditional, our relationship was untraditional and that made us different.

B.A.D.D HABITS 101: Trust your process. What works for one may not work for another. Shoes don't come one size fit all, so don't try to walk in anyone else's. While we all have a story, not everyone is willing to share theirs, and you don't know how long that person has had to wait or what they have had to go through for that breakthrough. Your time is coming—just keep pressing forward and working toward the prize. God's timing is perfect, and he knows how and when to supply your needs. I learned that things I thought I wanted or should have had weren't for me. This is my season, and I've now learned the true meaning of what God has for me: it is for me.

Safe

The year 2020 was a year of cleansing for me. The year brought many ups and downs, yet I choose to look at the year as half full instead of half empty. The devil tried to intervene, but my faith in God surpassed any plans or downfalls that tried to destroy me. Blessings come in many aspects, shapes, and forms. As unfortunate as COVID-19 has been, it has forced many businesses and educational facilities to get up to date with their technology and telecommunications.

The tongue is powerful. Speak life into the things you want. God is the supplier of your needs. As I was going into my last year at FAMU, finishing up my minor and major classes, things were getting interesting. The classes I needed were in the mornings and at odd times during the day. I worked full time, but a way had to be made. Still in this pandemic while things are different, my goals are more obtainable. I will never forget these most precious moments in my life because in them God favored me. This past year has been done with ease. I've been able to work from home, attend classes remotely, and not skip a beat. God has worked out all of the worries I once had of not being able to take classes due to the times or having to use up vacation time to attend classes.

Now in my final semester, all I can say is, "Thank you, Lord for covering me." The doors he has opened are still so unreal at times. As a wife, a mother, and a strong black woman I can proudly say I made it. The dream I had of graduating from FAMU, meeting my husband there, and having kids was achieved, although it happened much later and with the twist of a blended family. I am graduating with honors and I've already been accepted into graduate school at both Florida A&M University as well as Florida State University. What once seemed like such a bad time in my life I have transformed into a beautiful thing. The storms that were once drowning me I used to cleanse me. I am not allowing my past downfalls to define me. I'm turning all negativity into a positive.

Those bad habits I once had are now B.A.D.D (Building and Delivering Dreams) Habits. Now the CEO of the B.A.D.D HABIT t-shirt company, I've come up with this black-owned family business in hopes of this becoming something major for my team. No matter what comes of this, I'll always remember the motivation for it. I want my kids to know that they don't have to subject themselves to the labels of life; they can simply create their own.

To the person reading this book, thank you for sharing in my dreams. My hope is that my story inspires and encourages someone who might be experiencing defeat. Understanding that no one is perfect and that we all fall short and make mistakes is a real thing. Your past doesn't define you, and you only stay stuck if you keep yourself there. God gives his toughest battles to his strongest soldiers, so walk knowing that you are a conqueror. At the age of thirty-five, I'm fulfilling my purpose and living a meaningful life. I'm a B.A.D.D HABIT and I welcome you to be a B.A.D.D Habit-tee.

B.A.D.D HABITS 101: The familiar isn't always comfortable. While the unknown can be scary, it can also be rewarding. Don't be afraid to step out. A whole world of opportunity awaits you. This road hasn't been easy, but I can now proudly mark myself safe!